© 1998 Franklin Watts
96 Leonard Street
London
EC2A 4RH

Franklin Watts Australia
14 Mars Road
Lane Cove
NSW 2066

ISBN 0 7496 2979 7

Dewey Decimal Classification Number 690

A CIP catalogue record for this book is available from the British Library

Printed in Belgium

Editor: Samantha Armstrong
Art Director: Robert Walster
Designer: Diane Thistlethwaite
Illustrator: Teri Gower
Consultant: John Illingworth, Consultant in
Construction Methods and Technology

Picture credits: Chris Fairclough 20-21; Image Bank 6, 18, 24; J C Bamford Ltd.
cover, 8-9; QA Photos 14-15, 16-17; Robert Harding 12-13 (Ian Griffiths), 22-23
(Simon Harris), 27 (Robert Francis); Zefa 7.

MACHINES AT WORK

On a Building Site

W
FRANKLIN WATTS
NEW YORK • LONDON • SYDNEY

Buildings are everywhere.
All buildings begin
with a building site
and lots of machines.

The jaws of
this excavator
break up
the old building.

Sometimes old buildings
have to be knocked
down before new ones
can be built.

Dynamite is often used
to bring down
old buildings.

The ground needs to be flat before the new building starts. Excavators dig out any unwanted earth and load it into tipper trucks.

The bucket picks up the earth.

Wheelbarrows
can only move
a small amount
of earth at a time.

The excavator's
mechanical arm
is operated by
levers inside the cab.

Bulldozers spread
the earth and make
the ground flat.

This curved blade
pushes the earth
around.

Bulldozers have caterpillar tracks to help them move over the ground.

Some bulldozers are enormous.
They are powered by diesel motors.

Caterpillar track

When the ground is level, work can begin on the new building. Sometimes holes are drilled into the ground and filled with concrete.

This machine is drilling a deep hole for the foundations.

This helps to make a strong base, the foundations, for the building.

Often the foundations are made of concrete.

A hose is used to pour concrete into the right place.

Front-end loaders collect small stones to put under the concrete.

Stones and gravel
are tipped out of
the front-end
loader's bucket.

Lots of different materials are used on a building site - metal girders and metal sheets, bricks, stones, wood, pipes, sand, concrete, glass and tiles.

The concrete is mixed in the drum.

Special lorries carry ready-mixed concrete to the site.

Sometimes the materials
are delivered by lorry and
unloaded by forklift trucks.

Builders often move materials from one part of the site to another. Cranes lift and swing equipment across to where it is needed.

When the building is nearly finished, cranes are used to lower heavy objects into place.

Building workers use small machines as well as large ones. Carpenters and workmen have special tools to cut or shape different materials.

An electric sander makes wood smooth.

When the building work
is finished, other machines
are brought onto the site -
to scrub, clean and polish,
and prepare the building for use.

Cleaning machines
polish the floors.

27

Glossary

bulldozers push and spread material

cleaning machines polish floors

concrete mixer lorries carry ready-made concrete to the site

cranes lift and place materials

dynamite is used to bring buildings down

excavators dig and clear land

forklift trucks lift and move heavy objects

tipper trucks carry earth away

crane

cleaning machine

Index

concrete mixer lorry

wheelbarrow